Fall 2020

Rise Up

AN EIGHT WEEK STUDY OF PHILIPPIANS

DEBBIE AND PHIL WALDREP

EDITORIAL TEAM

Debbie Waldrep
Director, Women of Joy

Thomas Schwindling
Art Director, Women of Joy

Andi Pittman
Content Editor

Rise Up - Living Above Circumstances.
Choosing to Live with Joy.

Copyright © 2020 by Debbie and Phil Waldrep

Published in Decatur, Alabama by Women of
Joy. Women of Joy is a registered trademark of
Phil Waldrep Ministries.

ISBN 978-1-7323687-2-9

Printed in The United States of America

www.womenofjoy.org
www.philwaldrep.org

CONTENTS

Foreword 5

Introduction : Rise Up 9

Week One : See The Big Picture 12

Week Two : Make Godly Choices............................... 20

Week Three : Put Others First 26

Week Four : Be a Role Model 32

Week Five : Choose Joy... 40

Week Six : Pursue a Goal 48

Week Seven : Value Your Relationships 56

Week Eight : Finding Contentment............................ 64

Leader Guide 73

FOREWORD

Every Women of Joy conference seeks to make an eternal difference in the life of every person that attends. The speakers, musicians and special guests all share in our aim.

While many wonderful things happen at these events, there is nothing like the lasting impact of studying God's Word. It comforts us, challenges us and convicts us.

This "Rise Up" Bible study explores the Book of Philippians through the eyes of a woman in the church at Philippi. The issues she faced are the same as ours. Culture, technology and communication might be different, but the struggles are the same.

I encourage you to find a quiet place, get your Bible and a pen, and ask our Heavenly Father to speak to you as you work through these pages.

Please know that my husband, Phil, and I are praying for you as you study. We agree with the Apostle Paul when he wrote in Philippians 1:6, "And I am sure of this, that he who began a good work in you will bring it to completion at the day of Jesus Christ."

Debbie Waldrep
Co-founder and Director
Women of Joy

AN EIGHT WEEK STUDY
OF PHILIPPIANS

RISE UP

"I thank my God in all remembrance of you, always in every prayer of mine for you all making my prayer with joy..."

Philippians 1:3-4

Euodia sat outside her home, staring into the distance. Sitting outside staring was her daily routine that gave her some "me" time before her day would be occupied with the needs of two emotional teenagers, a demanding husband and a noisy neighbor.

She enjoyed these early mornings alone with her thoughts remembering the blessings of life and expressing her praise in silent prayer to her Heavenly Father. These quiet moments kept life in perspective.

But today was different.

She couldn't find the words to express how she felt. Depressed? No, that wasn't the right word.

Discouraged felt a little closer to her emotional state but it, too, fell short of a proper description.

Was she unfulfilled? Unhappy? Overwhelmed?

Every word that came to her mind seemed to be a partial description but didn't adequately describe how she felt. Maybe, she thought, the best word was "different."

She remembered a time when every day was an adventure. She felt good, her friends were many and church was the highlight of her week. These were the days when, it seemed, life couldn't get any better.

But something had changed.

Now, for Euodia, life was routine. It was an existence with an occasional ray of sunshine.

Church was an obligation rather than a joy. Drama often characterized her relationships. She had more questions than answers about life.

In other words, life seemed overwhelming. She needed clarity, insight and encouragement.

What she needed was someone to speak into her life. Someone who would be straightforward and honest. Someone who loved and respected her. And someone who had impacted her life. Someone she admired.

Little did Euodia know that someone was about to step into her life again. Someone who would help her rise above her feelings and her struggles.

Which day? Sometimes? Which moment?

1. Evaluate your life right now. On a scale of 1 to 10, where would you rate your life?

SAD — 1 2 3 4 5 (6) 7 8 9 10 — HAPPY

EMPTY — 1 2 3 4 5 (6) 7 8 9 10 — FULFILLED

AIMLESS — 1 2 3 4 5 (6) 7 8 9 10 — PURPOSEFUL

LONELY — 1 2 3 4 5 (6) 7 8 9 10 — CONNECTED

2. What circumstances, if they changed, do you feel would allow you to have the life you have always wanted?

1) Closer walk w/ Jesus
Better understanding of his word

3. Place a check next to the things that you (honestly) think bring people the greatest joy?

_____ Health   _____ Money   ✓ Jesus
_____ Spouse   _____ Friends   ✓ Church
_____ Children   _____ Job   _____ Car
_____ House   _____ Family   _____ Relationships

1 | SEE THE BIG PICTURE

"And I am sure of this, that he who began a good work in you will bring it to completion at the day of Jesus Christ."

Philippians 1:6

"I entreat Euodia and I entreat Syntyche..."

Philippians 4:2

Euodia is a real person in history. She is mentioned once in the Bible in Philippians 4:2. We don't know anything about her background or family. Yet the one time she is mentioned tells us that she was a believer, was a part of the church at Philippi and was someone who had struggled.

Like many of us, Euodia was trying to make sense of everything that was happening to her emotionally and spiritually.

- Why were bad things happening to her and to people she loved?
- Why were the things she assumed about God being challenged?
- Was God now the same loving, powerful Heavenly Father she had discovered when she gave her life to Jesus?

She wasn't alone in her thoughts. Unknown to her, many of her friends were feeling and thinking the same way.

Her doubts, along with the questions of her friends, concerned their pastor, Epaphroditus. He, too, probably was wondering the same things.

So, Epaphroditus decided to visit Paul in prison to discuss their concerns. Paul, in turn, wrote a long letter to Euodia and her church family in Philippi. That letter is Philippians in the Bible.

To understand this epistle and the questions it answers, you must remember how the church started.

The Holy Spirit sent Paul and Silas to Philippi and the surrounding areas to share the gospel. When they arrived for the first time, the two men found only a few women praying by a river.

The preaching of Paul and Silas resulted in one of the ladies, Lydia, and a demon-possessed girl becoming Christians. Although it is impossible to know, Euodia possibly was there too.

As a result, the leaders put Paul and Silas in jail. While in jail, an earthquake occurred that resulted in the salvation of the jailer and his family. Together, the women, the jailer and his family formed the church in Philippi.

> **1. Read Acts 16:25-34. Why do you feel the earthquake occurred, setting Paul and Silas free? How do you think the jailer and his family would have responded if there had been no earthquake?**

Time passed. Now, Paul was in prison again for preaching the gospel. This time he was in Rome. It was natural for the believers in Philippi to ask, "why doesn't God send another earthquake to set him free?"

Did Paul have a lack of faith? Or was there a sin in his life keeping him from having victory over his circumstances? Did God still love Paul?

2. Can you understand why Euodia and the other Christians in Philippi might have asked these questions? What circumstances do you have in your life that are causing you to ask similar questions? Briefly write about them here.

Paul reminded them that none of these assumptions were true. Instead, he wanted them to see that our Heavenly Father has a bigger plan – a plan for people to hear the gospel and to have a personal relationship with Christ.

Paul's message was simple: to rise above the negative experiences of life and view them through the "big picture" of God's plan.

Life, for the moment, might be painful. Relationships might be strained. Tomorrow may not be as promising as yesterday. Yet our Lord is working in you and through you – just like Paul – to impact the world around you.

3. Read Romans 8:28. Which of these phrases correctly completes the statement below:

Some Things   Few Things   All Things

"And we know that for those who love God _____ work together for good; for those who are called according to his purpose". (ESV)

4. Read Philippians 1:12 and summarize in your own words the purpose Paul saw in what was happening to him.

"I want you to know, brothers, that what has happened to me has really _____."

Yes, God used an earthquake in Acts 16 to establish the church in Philippi. In that case, setting Paul and Silas free had the greatest impact for the gospel.

Now, Paul's imprisonment was having an impact too. Paul mentioned two ways being a prisoner was influencing others and accomplishing God's plan.

5. Read Philippians 1:13. Fill in the blank in this sentence.

God was accomplishing His plan ("the big picture") by Paul's imprisonment because the _____ heard the gospel. (Hint: This was a specific group of people employed by the Roman government.)

One way that the Romans made sure prisoners didn't escape was by chaining a guard to the prisoner. The guard would stay there for four hours, then another guard would take his place.

Can you imagine the conversations Paul had with each of his guards? Paul always shared the gospel. When Paul and his guards would walk around and talk with members of government, Paul again shared the gospel. As a result, many of the guards and political leaders became Christians. An earthquake couldn't have had the impact of these long conversations.

6. Read Philippians 1:14. Check each of these phrases that describe the effect Paul's time in prison had on other believers.

_____They were bolder in witnessing.

_____They were stronger in their faith.

_____They assumed leadership in Paul's absence.

All the above occurred. Believers, seeing the boldness of Paul while in prison, were bolder in their witnessing. As a result, they were stronger in their walk with God.

One other result Paul mentioned was the leadership roles people were assuming in his absence.

Paul was a strong leader. Often, Christians and church leaders let Paul and his co-workers do the preaching, teaching and witnessing. But with Paul in prison, a void existed. Paul's faithfulness and courage convicted them to begin preaching boldly and assuming leadership in the church.

As a human, prison wasn't fun for Paul. It wasn't pleasant. But Paul knew God was working even when he couldn't see the plan clearly.

7. Think about your life presently. What are some ways you think God can use your "unpleasant circumstances" to impact others with the gospel?

FURTHER STUDY: Take a moment to review the life of Joseph, Jacob's son, in the Old Testament. Reflect on all the bad things that happened to him: (1) His brothers sold him into slavery (Genesis 37:12-36), (2) He went to prison for something he did not do (Genesis 39:1-12), and (3) A friend he helped forgot about him when he could have returned the favor (Genesis 40:20-23). But Joseph never lost faith in God because he knew God was working to fulfill something big in his life. Read Genesis 45:1-15 to see what Joseph said about the plan God had for his life.

Now, list the bad things that have happened to you. Can you list ways God already has used them for good? What do you think is something big God ultimately is going to fulfill in your life?

2 | MAKE GODLY CHOICES

"For to me to live is Christ, and to die is gain."

Philippians 1:21

Have you ever stopped to consider how your thoughts affect you and the people around you?

Discouragement, for example, feeds discouragement. When one person starts to talk about "how bad things are," some others join the lament. When one person becomes convinced things aren't going to get better, others become convinced as well.

On the other hand, encouragement feeds encouragement. Optimism increases optimism.

Yet optimism or pessimism begins with a choice – a choice of where to focus our thoughts.

Remember the old slogan "an optimist sees the glass half-full and a pessimist sees it half-empty?" Well, it is true. You see and do what you choose to see and do.

All of us often dwell on the decisions we regret, but it is helpful to think about the good choices you have made in your life.

1. Take a moment and think about the choices you have made. Make a list of five choices you made that have impacted your life in a positive way.

1.

2.

3.

4.

5.

The believers who worshiped in Philippi were committed but discouraged. Circumstances, particularly Paul's imprisonment, robbed their joy in life. Many of the believers, including Euodia, probably thought joy would return if circumstances changed.

Paul used his own experience to illustrate a powerful truth for a believer. Joy isn't based on what is happening around us. It is based on our relationship with Christ. Therefore, if you wish to rise above your circumstances, choose joy regardless of what life offers you.

As Paul sat in a Roman prison, there appeared to be little reason to rejoice. So, Paul spent his time thinking about the ways the gospel was changing people and the world. He chose to focus on something spiritually profitable.

2. This may take a few minutes, but it is worth it. Open your Bible to the Book of Philippians. Quickly scan through the four chapters of this book and mark every time you find the word joy. How many "joys" did you find? Write your answer here: _____ times.

Paul had a secret to choosing joy. He realized that he was in a "win-win" situation.

3. Read Philippians 1:21 and fill in the blanks.
"For to me to _____ is Christ, and to _____ is gain."

When Paul wrote these words, his future was uncertain. Any day he could be tried and executed for preaching the gospel. If he was died, Paul would be free from the problems of life and would start enjoying heaven for all eternity. On the other hand, if he lived, Paul could continue teaching, preaching and sharing Jesus. Either way, he won!

When a person finds happiness in what is happening around them, their joy is short-lived. Circumstances change. People move to another city. Businesses close. Disaster happens.

But when a person finds their joy in their walk with Jesus, nothing can take it away. With Christ as the source of their joy, they can rise above any situation. It is unchangeable because He is unchanging.

4. Think about people in your life – past or present – who went through a horrible experience but never lost their joy. Write here who it was and how it affected you.

When people lose their joy, it affects their attitude and actions. Discouraged people (i.e. people living without joy) often make bad choices. The results have lasting negative implications. That is why Paul reminded believers like Euodia in Philippi to choose to walk "worthy of the gospel."

To understand Paul's meaning, think of a high school volleyball team. A young student tries out for the team, hoping she makes it. The day comes when the coach announces who made the team. Her name is called, and she is presented a uniform. Then, speaking to the whole team, the coach reminds them they now represent their school. He encourages them not to do anything on or off the court to dishonor the ones they represent. Likewise, Paul encourages the believers to live in a way that honors the gospel at all times.

5. Read each of these situations people often face. Write the way a believer should respond if they are to "walk worthy of the gospel."

When someone lies about you –

When someone else gets the job/promotion –

When someone cuts you off in traffic –

When you are tempted –

"Walking worthy of the gospel" is more than good reactions. It is intentional choices or actions we take. It affects how we relate to each other as believers.

6. Read Philippians 1:27. Using the verse as a guide, fill in the blanks to see how Paul said believers should act towards each other.

Paul said that we should be united in _____, having one _____ and we should be _____ together for the faith of the gospel.

7. Make a list of things you can do to keep your church unified and centered on Christ. Some of them should be things you do on a regular basis (i.e. praying for others). Some will be things you can do occasionally (i.e. writing a thank you note).

Our Heavenly Father wants you to remember what Paul taught the Philippians. Whether you rise above your circumstances or whether they rob you of your joy, depends on what you choose to do. Everyone may be sad or discouraged for brief times. If, however, you commit to constantly choose joy, you can rise above them every time.

FURTHER STUDY: For three years, the disciples lived with Jesus and learned from Him. After the resurrection, they were uncertain of their future. In their minds, it would be impossible to do ministry without the physical presence of Jesus. The early Christians thought the same about Paul. Read Acts 1:1-11 and note the specific instructions Jesus gave his disciples to follow after his ascension.

3 | PUT OTHERS FIRST

"Do nothing from selfish ambition or conceit, but in humility count others more significant than yourselves."

Philippians 2:3

When you read the Bible, it is easy to assume everyone mentioned there was perfect or close to it. You see all the good things they did without seeing the bad.

You possibly see biblical characters, especially those serving in the New Testament church, as people without the struggles and problems you have. You may think that Euodia was a woman with spiritual depth, who lived without problems and was liked by everyone.

Euodia, however, was a person like you. She found it hard to praise the Lord when things weren't going well. She probably continued serving in church when she didn't physically feel like doing so. And she probably had her share of personality conflicts with other people.

We can make those assumptions because Euodia was a fallen, sinful human being who found forgiveness in Jesus Christ. She loved her Lord and His church, but she wasn't perfect.

One area where Euodia struggled (as we will see in a later chapter) was relationships. She wasn't the only one. When people get discouraged and lose joy, it often reveals itself first in your interactions with others.

1. Below is a list of signs people who have unhealthy relationships might exhibit. Circle the ones that apply to you.

Trying to please everyone

Unable to say no

Needing to express an opinion

Arguing

Refusing to acknowledge someone

Having a friend solely to yourself

Allowing others to manipulate you

Trying to get your way

Intentionally leaving someone out

Trying to get even

As a believer, it is easy to hide your feelings or actions towards other Christians but act like everything is fine. Before long, however, our hearts become toxic and others begin to see our real feelings.

2. Paul gave the principle that should guide our actions regarding others, especially in the church. It is found in Philippians 2:3. Fill the blanks below.

"Do nothing from _____ or _____, but in _____ count others more _____ than yourselves." (ESV)

Paul mentioned two motivations that you should avoid – being competitive with others and helping others for the wrong reason.

Rivalry often means selfish ambition or strife in the Bible. It refers to people performing or competing. For example, if someone wants to sing just to prove they are a good singer or that they can sing better than someone else, that is the type of selfish ambition that Paul condemned.

Conceit or vainglory means you allow your actions to be motivated by approval or applause of people. It is easy to see how conceit would affect someone who is teaching or singing, but it also affects people who help the poor or visit senior adults.

Paul earlier condemned preachers who were preaching for "envy and rivalry" (See Philippians 1:17). Both rivalry and conceit are selfish motivations. The focus is on us. They may give us a temporary sense of importance but never give us lasting joy.

> **3. Why does competition and seeking applause never give us lasting joy? Can you think of examples of people who you feel serve for the right reasons? How do they differ from those who don't? Write your thoughts here.**

In contrast to conceit and selfish ambition, Paul stated that Christians should put others first with humility.

In the first century, humility was a negative trait, not a positive virtue. People used the word to describe the mentality of a slave. It described someone who had no value in society or lesser value than someone else. In the mind of a slave, her owner was more valuable than she.

As a Christian, you shouldn't view yourself as having no value. You do! Nor should we neglect our needs. We shouldn't!

As C.S. Lewis wrote in Mere Christianity, "humility is not thinking less of yourself, but thinking of yourself less." That is why Paul told the church at Philippi "Let each of you look not only to his own interests, but also to the interests of others" (Philippians 2:4).

Paul assumed a healthy Christian would care for herself, but a humble believer moves beyond her own needs to help meet the needs of others.

Humility is treating others like you want to be treated. It refuses to gossip or put others down. It brags on others, even people you dislike. It encourages and builds others up. Humility allows others to be in the spotlight instead of yourself.

> 4. Our culture, like the first century, doesn't value humility as a positive trait in our lives. Yet we admire people who are humble. Why do you feel it isn't viewed positively? Can a person be strong and humble? If so, how?

Paul gave a wonderful example of someone who put others first – our Lord Jesus Christ.

> 5. In Philippians 2:5-8, Paul describes the humility Jesus demonstrated for us. After reading these verses, complete the following list of things Jesus did:
>
> 1. He left _____ to come to earth.
>
> 2. He became a _____.
>
> 3. Jesus took the form of a _____.
>
> 4. He was willing to die on a _____.

The willingness of Jesus to come to earth and die so that we could live eternally is the ultimate act of selflessness and humility.

Jesus put you first and endured the shame of crucifixion. He put you first and endured the pain of the cross.

Jesus put you first and paid your sin debt with his sacrifice. He put you first and rose again so you could have eternal life.

Jesus' actions prove that putting others first allows you to rise above whatever is happening in your life.

> FURTHER STUDY: John 19 is a powerful description of the crucifixion of Jesus. Read it carefully. On a piece of paper write phrases or words that you find in these verses that describe the humiliation Jesus experienced. Then make a list of the times Jesus could have (and most of us would have) stopped the proceedings and put Himself first. What did you discover about how you should act when others don't deserve your selflessness or acts of humility?

4 | BE A ROLE MODEL

"But you know Timothy's proven worth, how as a son with a father he has served with me in the gospel."

Philippians 2:22

Several years ago, a basketball coach realized some of her players were making bad decisions. Although she encouraged them to do otherwise, it appeared only her comments on the basketball court affected their behavior. Then an idea occurred to her.

The next day, instead of their usual practice, the coach told them they were going to visit the elementary school. There, the players interacted with the young children who treated them like stars. The children asked for their autographs, wanted to have their pictures taken with the players, and stared at them as though they were famous. The team was shocked at how the young kids admired them.

Before the team left, the principal of the elementary school thanked the players for coming. Then she added, "I hope you all remember that everything you do is being watched by these children. You are their role models and I hope you never disappoint them."

The experiment worked. The attitude and actions of the players changed.

As a Christian, you are a role model. Younger believers are watching how you act. Other church members are taking their cues from you. Your actions affect the people around you.

When you see yourself as an influencer, you often think before you act. You seek to make a positive impression rather than reinforce or encourage bad behavior.

1. Quickly make a list of the names of people you see every day. Think of your family, neighbors, co-workers or friends. Beside each name, on a scale of 1 to 10 (1 being weakest, 10 being the strongest), how would you rate the influence you have on that person? Now put another number by their name indicating the amount of influence they have on you. Do you think these people see how much they influence you

Euodia, the lady mentioned in the book of Philippians, probably failed to see how much of a role model she was. Odds are, neither did any of her friends. That is why Paul called the believers in Philippi "lights in the world" (Philippian 2:15).

You probably think of a bad role model as someone who makes a life-changing bad decision. Certainly, a person who abuses alcohol or drugs, engages in immoral behavior, or holds racist views will have a negative effect on their children or their friends.

Being a positive role model is more than life-alternating positive decisions. It often is the "little things" you do.

Paul mentioned two kinds of verbal expressions that set a positive role model apart from a negative one: grumbling and arguing (Philippians 2:14).

Grumbling or complaining is expressing a lack of trust in people. It is stating that someone else isn't being fair or they are failing to do their part. Grumbling is verbalizing your dissatisfaction with others.

Arguing is complaining taken one step further. It is trying to force people to conform to your ideas or your perception of fairness.

Complaining and arguing keep people at an emotional distance and, in some cases, destroy relationships. It certainly affects the spirit of the church.

On the contrary, believers should restrain their tongue and speak only words of encouragement and affirmation. The words from the mouth of a Christian should build up, not tear down.

2. Do a "word inventory". For the next 24 hours, keep a sheet of paper handy or take notes on your phone. Every time you complain or grumble about something, (i.e. someone cut you off in traffic, a customer was rude, etc.) write it down the first time you get a chance. Tomorrow, look at your list. Did you find yourself consciously not complaining because you knew you would have to note it? How did your negative comments, even spoken to yourself, affect your day?

3. Do another "word inventory" during the next 24 hours. This time keep a record of every kind or positive word you said about someone or something. How did your positive words affect your outlook on life? How did it change how you viewed people? How did it make you feel about yourself?

When Paul wrote letters to a church like Philippi, he often gave examples so they could see a demonstration of what he was saying.

Earlier, Paul cited Jesus as the best example of someone who put others first. In closing the second chapter of Philippians, he gave three examples of someone who "practiced what he preached."

First Paul mentioned himself. He wasn't arrogant or egotistical when he said he was like a drink offering poured onto a sacrifice (Philippians 2:17).

In the Old Testament, a drink offering was a liquid poured onto a sacrifice after it was offered to the Lord. The drink offering would turn to steam almost immediately. Unlike the burnt sacrifice, the drink offering was consumed totally.

Paul used the picture of the drink offering as an expression of someone being totally committed to Christ. It included his willingness to die for his Lord.

4. Circle the following words that describe someone who is "totally committed.":

Careless	Distracted	Gossiper
Focused	Selfless	Encourager
Disciplined	Complainer	Dedicated

The two other examples Paul gave were Timothy (Philippians 2:19-24) and Epaphroditus (Philippians 2:25-30), two people the Philippian believers knew well. They stood in contrast to the selfishness of complainers and grumblers.

Paul identified three ways that Timothy and Epaphroditus were role models to follow:

First, both were willing to go. Paul sent Timothy to Philippi to minister in his place while he was in prison. Epaphroditus was willing to go to Paul on behalf of the church, and he was willing to return to the church to minister with Timothy.

Travel between Philippi and Rome was difficult. It took days of traveling over poor roads. A person had to walk most of the way. In Epaphroditus' case, it meant he continued even when he was seriously ill.

Good Christian role models are willing to go with joy, while complainers seek ways to avoid doing anything.

> **5. Read Isaiah 6:1-8. What causes a person to be willing to "go" where the Lord wants them to go? Where is the Lord calling you to "go" or a place he is telling you to avoid?**

Timothy and Epaphroditus also had servant hearts. Paul noted both men served with him and ministered to his needs. A servant puts the needs of the one he or she is serving before his or her own desires.

6. What do each of these phrases mean to you?

Being a servant –

Having a servant's heart –

Finally, Paul noted how these two servants were willing to sacrifice for others, the church and the gospel.

7. Assuming Euodia was one of the "complainers" in the church, how do you think the examples of Timothy and Epaphroditus affected her? How do they affect you?

FURTHER STUDY: The children of Israel illustrate how complaining against the Lord, spiritual leaders and each other affects everything. Read Numbers 20:2-9 and Numbers 21:4-9. What effects did complaining have on the Israelites individually? Their families? Their nation? Read I Corinthians 10:1-11. What effects did Paul state their grumbling had on them individually? Their families? Their nation?

5 | CHOOSE JOY

"Finally, my brothers, rejoice in the Lord."

Philippians 3:1a

"Rejoice in the Lord always; again I will say, rejoice."

Philippians 4:4

Euodia was having "one of those days." She didn't feel well. She burned a meal because her child fell and injured his hand. Their donkey determined he didn't want anything on his back when she tried to go to the market. Now her husband is home, and he is irritated. Besides, it appears the vegetables she planted for food are going to die if it doesn't rain soon.

That evening she gathered with her family and friends to hear the letter Paul sent to their church. It was encouraging until she heard the words "rejoice in the Lord." How can a woman who had one of the worst days of her life rejoice?

1. Can you relate to the feelings of Euodia? On the scale below, rate the following time periods. (1=bad 10=great)

Rate this past day

1   2   3   4   5   6   7   8   9   10

Rate this past week.

1   2   3   4   5   6   7   8   9   10

Rate this past year.

1   2   3   4   5   6   7   8   9   10

Circumstances often affect your feelings about yourself, your family, your church, and your community. If you try to find your joy in what is happening around you, lasting joy will always elude you.

At least 18 times in Philippians, Paul wrote of joy or rejoicing, yet, he never mentioned happiness. Happiness is a modern expression that characterizes your life when everything is going well – you have a good job, your family is healthy, and relationships are at their best.

Joy is deeper. It is anchored to something unchanging and unmovable. Joy comes from knowing that God has everything under control, even when, from your own perspective, circumstances seem out of your control.

"If you cannot rejoice in your circumstances, you can always rejoice in the Lord who controls your circumstances," wrote Warren Wiersbe, a noted Bible teacher.

Epaphroditus, who was probably the one reading this letter to the church, was an example of someone who knew joy despite his feelings. Remember the words of Paul in Philippians 2:26-30? Epaphroditus almost died, yet, he had joy.

2. Think about the lives of the following people in the Bible. How did they find and express joy when their circumstances were unpleasant?

Moses –

Daniel –

Jonah –

Job –

Elisabeth –

Jesus –

When Paul told Euodia and the believers in her church to "rejoice in the Lord," he immediately warned them to avoid people and teachers who were negative. He called them dogs, evildoers and people who mutilate the flesh. Paul warned them to avoid people who taught that salvation or joy could be found anywhere outside of Christ.

Paul instructed Christians in finding the joy of the Lord.

To begin with, Christians need to remember who they are in Christ.

Paul wrote "we are the circumcision" (Philippians 3:3). Under the Jewish law, every male was to be circumcised eight days after birth. It was a symbol of the covenant Jehovah made with the Israelites. Every faithful Jew followed the practice.

Circumcision came to be viewed as proof of a relationship with God. Paul, however, wrote that only those who put their faith in Jesus have that relationship. In other words, you, as a believer, are a child of God.

3. Read Matthew 7:11. What promises are there for a child of God? How does this promise affect the bad things you are facing?

Worship should be your spiritual response to your relationship with Christ. (Philippians 3:3). It focuses your mind on the character of God. Your praise pleases Him, but it also helps you keep in perspective who He is and who you are.

4. Do you have a favorite song or hymn that draws you closer to God? Write the words to the song here. Take a moment to reflect on each phrase. Now, sing it to the Lord in worship.

Worship, in turn, prompts you to praise your Heavenly Father, knowing whatever comes into your life, He can handle it. That is why Paul told us to "glory in Christ Jesus" (Philippians 3:3). Maybe an illustration will help you understand the meaning of Paul's words:

Ella, a fourth-grade student, found herself bullied by a new student. Although the teacher tried to stop it, the bullying persisted. Ella heard the words but never responded. At times, it seems, she almost smiled in response.

Finally, the teacher asked her why the bullying didn't upset her. Ella replied, "Because I know something the new girl doesn't. My big sister has been sick, but she's coming back to school tomorrow. And she's big enough to handle it."

Ella understood that the words and actions weren't good. But she found security in knowing that her older sister could handle it.

The situations around you might be unpleasant or painful. People may wonder why you aren't falling apart. It is the same reason that Paul rejoiced when he was in prison. You have a Heavenly Father who can handle it!

> **5. Why do you feel God sometimes allows you to go through difficult situations? What are some lessons you learned when you were going through unpleasant experiences in the past?**

Paul gave one powerful instruction to the church. He said that no believer should put confidence in the flesh. That is, you should not rely on your own thoughts and feelings instead of the truth of God's Word.

To make his point, Paul shared his personal journey (Philippians 3:4-11). From his birth, he faithfully did what he thought and what he was told was right. Paul faithfully followed the Law of the Old Testament. He thought that would bring him eternal life and joy in the present one. It didn't.

Paul only found joy and a reason to rejoice when he gave his life to Christ. No authority, no person or any situation could take his joy away. His joy was found in Jesus.

> **6. Take a moment to read Galatians 5:22-23. How is joy a result of walking with God? How do prayer, Bible study, church attendance and worship affect your walk with the Lord?**

FURTHER STUDY: After years of captivity, Nehemiah returned to Jerusalem to rebuild the walls. He faced criticism, opposition, and delays. Every day brought a new struggle. Yet he remained faithful. Read Nehemiah 8:1-12. Mark the actions the Israelites took that affected their relationship with God and with each other. Read Nehemiah 8:10 again. What role did the joy of the Lord play in Nehemiah's life? What role did God want it to play in the believers' lives? What role does God want it to play in your life?

6 | PURSUE A GOAL

"I press on toward the goal for the prize of the upward call of God in Christ Jesus."

Philippians 3:14

When Euodia was a little girl, her mom probably gave her chores to do. Like little girls today, she probably asks her mom often, "why?" Many times, children ask why to find a reason not to fulfill the request. Most of the time, however, they are seeking a purpose for the activity.

As you grow older, the "what" becomes more important than the "why." Existence becomes an endless cycle of activities. Survival takes priority over purpose. Before long, life overwhelms you.

Joy comes from a life with purpose. People with a purpose succeed more, stress less and see setbacks as learning experiences. When they fall, they get up and start again.

1. Complete this sentence:

My goal in life is to _____

_____

_____.

As Paul wrote to the church at Philippi, he wanted them to see the significance of a purpose. To help them understand it, he used athletics as an illustration.

Olympic games (or games like them) were popular during Paul's life. In Ephesus, where Paul lived, there was an amphitheater that seated 100,000 people. Races with runners competing were popular.

Using the word picture of an athlete running, Paul stated that he "pressed on" in the Christian life. That is, he didn't allow anything to discourage or defeat him.

2. Think of your favorite competitive sport. How would you describe a perfect athlete in that sport? How would that athlete describe a perfect game? How does the discipline and training to become an athlete who has perfected that sport compare to the Christian life?

Paul stated his goal clearly in Philippians 3:14. He wanted to be mature in his faith and live a life that honored Christ. That was his purpose and it affected everything Paul did.

To help you have the same purpose, Paul clarified some necessary actions you must take.

3. Read Philippians 3:13. In your own words, complete these sentences:

Thinking about your past, Paul said you should

_____.

Thinking of your future, Paul said you should

_____.

Guilt may discourage you from living a joyful life. You remember past sins or poor decisions. You feel people view you with your past in mind. Yet Paul didn't allow his past to keep him from moving forward. Remember – Paul persecuted Christians. He stood approvingly as Stephen was stoned to death (Acts 7:54-60).

As sinners saved by grace, everyone has a sinful past. Satan wants to use it to discourage you from "pressing on" to be more like Jesus. That is why Paul encouraged believers to forget the sins God has forgiven.

> **4. The Bible uses powerful word pictures to demonstrate the forgiveness of God. Read each of these verses and write what your Heavenly Father did with your sins when He forgave you.**
>
> Psalm 103:12 –
>
>
> Isaiah 38:17 –
>
>
> Micah 7:19 –

Think of the power of each illustration found in these verses.

Psalm 103:12 informs you that God removed your sin as far as the east is from the west. If you started traveling north, eventually you would be headed south. If, on the other hand, you traveled east you would never be traveling west. Forgiveness means that your forgiven sins can never come before God again.

Isaiah described forgiveness using the human anatomy. God put your sins behind his back. If something is stuck between your shoulder blades, can you see it? Of course not.

Another description is found in Micah 7:19. The prophet said that God puts our sin in the depths of the sea. Corrie ten Boom often commented on this verse by adding, "And when he does, he posts a sign that reads 'No Fishing Allowed.'"

5. Write a prayer of gratitude to God for forgiving your sins. Try to think of another word picture you can use to express how you feel about forgiven sins.

Maturing as a believer isn't just about the past. It is about the future as well.

Paul described the future as doing one thing: he was going to continue growing his spiritual walk. His objective was to become more like Jesus every day.

The key to Paul's success, and yours, is to stay focused on the goal. Paul understood his over-arching purpose was to glorify God by following Jesus in everything he did. He used it as a filter to evaluate his actions, his words and his thoughts.

Paul knew distractions would come. After encouraging the Christians in Philippi to stay focused on the goal of glorifying God, he immediately warned them about people and things that would turn their eyes from the goal.

6. Read Hebrews 12:1-2. The writer of Hebrews also compared the Christian life to a runner in a race. To succeed, it is important for you to put away every distraction in your life that takes your eyes off Jesus. What are some things you need to consider putting out of your life to help you grow as a believer?

The Apostle included an appeal to mature Christians to help younger believers. He also encouraged all believers to find people stronger in their faith and more like Christ to follow as an example.

7. In Hebrews 12:1-2, the writer encourages you to look at the models of godliness in your life. Paul encouraged the same here. Who are some people that you view as mature, godly people? Why? How might you encourage them to spend more time with you and help you grow in your Christian life?

In setting the goal of maturing in the Christian life, Paul reminded the believers in Philippi of their heavenly citizenship. It was a concept they understood.

Philippi was a colony of Rome. The residents were Roman citizens. Rome, however, was far away. What they could or could not do was determined by leaders in an area far away.

As a believer, you live on earth, but you are a citizen of heaven. The words of Paul encourage you to remember who you are representing.

> 8. Read Philippians 3:20-21. Paul often mentions our bodies as temporary when encouraging spiritual maturity. How do your thoughts about your human body affect your spiritual maturity? How can an obsession with your body hinder your spiritual growth?

Believers should have one goal in life: to honor and glorify our Lord. When you do, it makes decisions easier. It helps you rise above painful situations. Putting Jesus first results in joy every time!

FURTHER STUDY: Forgetting isn't always about past sins. Sometimes it involves wrong priorities. Read Luke 9:57-62. What are some things people view as good, but they're things you left behind to follow Christ? How do you view those things now? Read Matthew 20:23-30. How do future rewards affect your commitment now? How should they?

7 | VALUE YOUR RELATIONSHIPS

"Let your reasonableness be known to everyone."

Philippians 4:5

Everyone needs relationships. You need people to love, and you need people to love you. You need people to encourage, and you need people to encourage you. Believers are stronger - collectively and individually - when they are supporting each other.

Maybe that is why Satan works the hardest to bring division between two people, especially Christians. When your church suffers from broken relationships, the effectiveness of your church weakens.

Euodia knew this was true. She probably encouraged people with wounded spirits to seek reconciliation. It is possible that she talked with young believers who were offended by words or actions of other Christians. Then, something happened.

1. How have you seen or heard of ways people get offended in church? How did it affect their lives and the effectiveness of the church?

Until now, this study let Euodia represent any woman in the early church who had the same struggles as others. In Philippians 4:2, however, Paul mentioned Euodia for the first and only time in the Bible.

Euodia and another woman in the church, Syntyche, had a conflict. Paul doesn't record the reason. Obviously, it wasn't a moral issue. Nor was it a questionable teaching. If it was, Paul would have confronted it directly.

Apparently, the conflict was a trivial, personal issue.

- Did Syntyche say something that hurt Euodia's family?
- Did Euodia neglect one of Syntyche's children in a school program?
- Did the two women disagree over a political issue?
- Was one trying to control the actions of the other?

Honestly, it is impossible to say.

There are a few things, however, Paul mentioned about these women.

First, they were believers. Paul affirmed their salvation as genuine when he wrote that their names were in the book of life (Philippians 4:3). The book of life (see Revelation 21:27) was a reference to people saved by grace and assured of a home in heaven.

Paul added that the two women worked with him and other church leaders to reach those who didn't know Christ. Paul also said that Euodia and Syntyche worked beside each other. In other words, there was a time when they encouraged and supported each other.

2. What are some areas where two Christians who love Christ can disagree? How can these disagreements cause friction between two people? What keeps people from agreeing to disagree on the minor things while they work together for the important things?

Paul appealed to each woman personally. He didn't prefer one over the other. Paul didn't imply which one was right about the issue and which one was wrong.

The church at Philippi started with a group of women praying on a riverbank. It was possible Euodia and Syntyche were two of these women. If so, they were influential in Lydia coming to Christ. They possibly helped the jailer and his family grow in their relationship with the Lord. Now something minor had grown into a conflict that was affecting the church.

3. Read Matthew 5:23-26. If you know someone is upset because of something you did, what are you to do? If you are upset with someone for something they did, what are you to do? Of the two sentences below, circle the one that is true.

1. Regardless of what I did or what they did, it is the other person's responsibility to come to me first.

2. Regardless of what I did or what they did, it is my responsibility to make the first move toward forgiveness and reconciliation.

To solve the conflict, Paul appealed for each woman to "agree in the Lord". Believers have a common ground in Christ. They share the same values. Their goals of being the body of Christ are the same. Christians may disagree about methods or personalities, but they should be able to find common ground without making matters worse.

Paul also appealed to the others in the church. Instead of taking sides, they should try to help the reconciliation. Paul possibly was appealing to a friend of both women, maybe Lydia. Or he could have been appealing to a church leader they both respected. Regardless of who Paul meant, it was the responsibility of every church member to help.

4. Do you know two believers who have experienced conflict? What are some ways you could help the two reconcile with each other?

It clearly is the will of God for believers to restore broken relationships whenever possible. It is also important to value relationships by making every possible effort to avoid painful conflict in the future.

After Paul urged Euodia and Syntyche to reconcile, he turned his attention again to the intentional act of rejoicing. Then Paul gave instructions for relating to people.

Paul knew broken relationships affect a person's joy and their ability to rise above their circumstances. That is why the Bible encourages believers to value every relationship.

5. Read Philippians 4:5. Paul told the Philippians to let their "reasonableness" be known to everyone. Circle the words below that describe a reasonable person?

Patient	Kind	Listener
Argumentative	Thoughtful	Understanding
Gossiper	Sensitive	Selfish

Paul included an appeal to pray. To help them value their friendships, Paul encouraged all the believers in Philippi to pray with thanksgiving.

6. How does thanking God for the good qualities of the people in your life help you minimize areas of conflict?

FURTHER STUDY: Sometimes conflicts between Christians are so deep it is difficult for them to work together. A disagreement over methods, music, or outreach cannot be reached. A disagreement over where to do a ministry or who should be involved might force two believers to do ministry in different ways, in different places, and with different people. Scan Acts chapters 13, 14 and 15. Read Acts 15:36-41. What differences did Paul and Barnabas have? Why? How did they deal with their difference of opinion? Was the church stronger or weaker because of their willingness to address their differences with love and support?

8 | FINDING CONTENTMENT

"Not that I am speaking of being in need, for I have learned in whatever situation I am to be content."

Philippians 4:11

Paul was a leader who spoke truth even when it hurt. His honest appeal to Euodia and Syntyche came from a heart of love. They respected Paul and, more than likely, reconciled their differences. When two believers love Christ and their church, they are willing to set aside their opinions and personal preferences for the sake of the gospel.

Paul knew the secret to rising above any situation was setting pride aside. Conflicts occur when selfishness enters any relationship. When you demand your way, others will demand their way. Healthy relationships happen when you put others before your own desires.

After addressing Euodia and Syntyche, Paul turned his attention to the emotional effect of pride. Pride tells you that you can do anything. When you realize you can't, worry and anxiety takes over.

For that reason, Paul instructed believers to pray about everything and the peace of God would fill their hearts.

1. Make a list of everything worry achieves (if you can think of one!). Now make a list of everything you witnessed prayer achieving. How does anxiety or worry take away peace? How does prayer calm our hearts?

The battle over worry lives in our hearts (emotions) and our minds (thoughts). One affects the other. If you think about the negative things that can happen, worry occurs. If you worry, then you think only about the negative things that can happen. It becomes an endless cycle.

Paul knew you had more control over your thoughts than you may think. That is why he listed eight things to occupy our thoughts in Philippians 4:8-9.

Godly thoughts dwell on what is true. Worry thinks only about rumors.

Godly thoughts dwell on what is honest and honorable, especially about yourself. Negative thoughts repeat lies about your sins and who you are in Christ.

Godly thoughts dwell on what is just. Anger thinks only of getting even.

Godly thoughts dwell on purity. Lust dwells on impure thoughts and ideas.

Godly thoughts dwell on what is lovely. Anxiety sees the "what ifs" in everything.

Godly thoughts dwell on the commendable and good in others. Jealousy thinks only of getting its way and repeating gossip.

The last two things Paul mentioned relate to thoughts that turn your heart to praising God. When you see things that have excellence, you see your blessings. When you think of things that are worthy of praise, you express it to your Heavenly Father.

2. How do negative thoughts or impure thoughts affect you and your actions?

Paul concludes his words to Euodia and the church at Philippi by urging them to learn contentment.

Modern society often doesn't view contentment as a virtue. They see it as lacking motivation or wanting to improve. Paul, however, saw contentment as rejecting selfishness and the things that go with it.

As a believer, you should try to improve your skills and abilities to be and do the best you can. Your motive, however, should be to honor the Lord and to have the ability to share the gospel with others.

Contentment is the opposite of greed and envy. It is the opposite of thinking everyone owes you something or you are entitled to it.

Contentment allows you to rejoice when others are blessed. It gives you the ability to say "no" to debt. Contentment gives you strength to resist temptation regarding material possessions.

3. Paul spoke of times when he had plenty and times when he didn't. Write a brief summary of a time when you struggled financially, and write about a time when you had plenty. What did you learn from both situations?

Contentment to Paul wasn't a mental exercise. It doesn't come naturally. Instead, being contented is something you learn. It comes from experiences and spiritual growth.

Paul shared his secret in Philippians 4:13. He could "do all things through him who strengthens me." Paul's secret wasn't self-reliance but a total dependence in his Lord.

Many people take Paul's words to mean they can literally do anything they set their minds to do. If you interpret it that way, you miss what Paul taught. The limitless source of power available in Christ give you the ability to do the things you should do and the ability to do the things you are called to do.

4. Make a list of the things you need to do to be a successful Christ follower. As you make your list, remember there are some things you might need that aren't tangible, such as patience. Be sure to include them.

5. Complete this sentence:

"I believe God is calling me to _____

_____.

Now make a list of the things you need to fulfill this calling.

One sign of a content and mature Christian is a willingness to share. Giving pleases God. It meets the needs of others. For the giver, it allows spiritual growth to occur.

Paul described the gifts the church in Philippi gave to him as "a fragrant offering, a sacrifice acceptable and pleasing to God" (Philippians 4:18).

6. What are the benefits of giving? How has God blessed you, and how have you grown spiritually by giving?

Paul concludes his letter to Euodia and the other believers in Philippi by giving them a promise to claim: God provides everything you need to do His will. This promise has specific wording. It is "according to" and not "out of" his riches in glory. That is, the promise doesn't provide everything you want or think you need. Instead, it provides everything you need to honor and glorify Him!

The theme of this study is "Rise Up." Paul's letter to the Philippians and to the individuals like Euodia in the church was to assure them that they could rise above every situation.

7. As you conclude this study, what is an area where you feel you need to "rise up" and spiritually overcome? What have you discovered in this study that will help you do it?

FURTHER STUDY: God has a plan for your life. He has given you gifts, skills and abilities to fulfill His calling. The Bible often calls these "talents." Read Matthew 25:14-29. Write this parable in modern day language using a skill or ability that you have in place of "talents." Read your story. What do you sense the Holy Spirit is speaking to you? Read Luke 16:1-13. Write this parable in modern language as well. What do you sense the message of this story is? What does the passage say to you about worldly possessions? Is the Lord prompting you to make any personal decisions in this area?

LEADER GUIDE

1. Read Acts 16:25-34. Why do you feel the earthquake occurred, setting Paul and Silas free? How do you think the jailer and his family would have responded if there had been no earthquake?

Answers may vary. This question is to remind members of your group that while we do not control our circumstances, God can use any circumstance for his good.

2. Can you understand why Euodia and the other Christians in Philippi might have asked these questions? What circumstances do you have in your life that are causing you to ask similar questions? Briefly write about them here:

Depending on the size of the group, you may want to limit each person's time to share to five minutes or less. Or you may feel led to allow the group to spend the majority of the time on these opening questions. Be sensitive to the Holy Spirit.

3. Read Romans 8:28. Which of these phrases correctly completes the statement below:

"And we know that for those who love God all things work together for good; for those who are called according to his purpose." (ESV)

4. Read Philippians 1:12 and summarize in your own words the purpose Paul saw in what was happening to him.

"I want you to know, brothers, that what has happened to me has really served to advance the gospel."

5. Read Philippians 1:13. Fill in the blank in this sentence:

God was accomplishing His plan ("the big picture") by Paul's imprisonment because the <u>Imperial Guard</u> heard the gospel.

6. Read Philippians 1:14. Check each of these phrases that describe the effect Paul's time in prison had on other believers.

All of the above occured. Paul's impact on those around him made them bolder in their faith.

7. Think about your life presently. What are some ways you think God can use your "unpleasant circumstances" to impact others with the gospel?

Answers may vary. Remember to encourage members of your group that while seasons may be hard, if they weather the storm, their testimonies can be tools for God to use to change the lives of others.

1. Take a moment and think about the choices you have made. Make a list of five choices you have made that have impacted your life in a positive way.

Answers will vary. Use this as an ice breaker for your group to build a foundation for the rest of the discussion.

2. This may take a few minutes, but it is worth it. Open your Bible to the book of Philippians. Quickly scan through the four chapters of this book and mark every time you find the word joy.

The words "Joy" and "Rejoice" are used sixteen times in the book of Philippians. Remind your group members the circumstances under which Paul wrote this epistle and the importance of Paul's joy in his situation.

3. Read Philippians 1:21 and fill in the blanks.

"For to me to <u>live</u> is Christ, and to <u>die</u> is gain."

4. Think about people in your life – past or present – who went through a horrible experience but never lost their joy. Write here who it was and how it affected you.

Answers will vary. This question is designed to create some deep reflection. Keep in mind that the topics brought up in this discussion may still be tender subjects to those who are sharing.

5. Read each of these situations that people often face. Write the way a believer should respond if they are to "walk worthy of the gospel."

Answers will vary.

6. Read Philippians 1:27. Using the verse as a guide, fill in the blanks to see how Paul said believers should act towards each other.

Paul said that we should be united in spirit, having one mind and we should be striving together for the faith of the gospel.

1. Below is a list of signs people who have unhealthy relationships might exhibit. Circle the ones that apply to you.

Answers will vary. This question helps set the stage for further conversation about this topic. Encourage group members to stay away from discussing particular relationships that they may find unhealthy.

2. Paul gave the principle that should guide our actions regarding others, especially in the church. It is found in Philippians 2:3. Fill the blanks below.

"Do nothing from <u>selfish ambition</u> or <u>conceit</u>, but in <u>humility</u> count others more <u>significant</u> than yourselves." (ESV)

3. Why does competition and seeking applause never give us lasting joy? Can you think of examples of people who you feel serve for the right reasons? How do they differ from those who don't? Write your thoughts here:

Answers will vary. As participants share, encourage them to share their examples of people who serve for the right reasons. Often remembering those who serve well drives us to be more like them.

4. Our culture, like the first century, doesn't value humility as a positive trait in our lives. Yet we admire people who are humble. Why do you feel it isn't viewed positively? Can a person be strong and humble? If so, how?

Answers will vary. This question is a great conversation starter on the tension between strength and humility. As participants share, remind them that the two can live in harmony as long as our strength comes from the Lord.

5. In Philippians 2:5-8, Paul describes the humility Jesus demonstrated for us. After reading these verses, complete the following list of things Jesus did:

1. He left heaven to come to earth.
2. He became a human.
3. Jesus took the form of a servant.
4. He was willing to die on a cross.

1. Quickly make a list of the names of people you see every day. Think of your family, neighbors, co-workers or friends. Beside each name, on a scale of 1 to 10 (1 being weakest, 10 being the strongest), how would you rate the influence you have on that person? Now put another number by their name indicating the amount of influence they have on you. Do you think these people see how much they influence you?

This is a great icebreaker to open up discussion about influence and how members of your group use it. Encourage honest discussion about the importance of being a role model to those around them.

2. Do a "word inventory". For the next 24 hours, keep a sheet of paper handy or take notes on your phone. Every time you complain or grumble about something, (i.e. someone cut you off in traffic, a customer was rude, etc.) write it down the first time you get a chance. Tomorrow, look at your list. Did you find yourself consciously not complaining because you knew you would have to note it? How did your negative comments, even spoken to yourself, affect your day?

3. Do another "word inventory" during the next 24 hours. This time keep a record of every kind or positive word you said about someone or something. How did your positive words affect your outlook on life? How did it change how you viewed people? How did it make you feel about yourself?

These two questions are designed to create some deep reflection. They will require the people in your group to do a self inventory on how much negativity and positivity they bring to their own lives. If your group is well-connected, consider encouraging a buddy system of accountability so each person does the exercises. Encourage them to share a report the next time you meet.

4. Circle the following words that describe someone who is "totally committed":

Depending on where members of your group are in their walk with The Lord, their views of total commitment may differ from one another. Remind them that the example that Paul used of total commitment required offerings to be completely consumed.

5. Read Isaiah 6:1-8. What causes a person to be willing to "go" where the Lord wants them to go? Where is the Lord calling you to "go" or a place he is telling you to avoid?

Again – group members' answers my differ depending on where members of your group are in their personal faith.

6. What do each of these phrases mean to you?

Answers will vary. Remind group members that those who have a servants heart are often humble, joyful servants.

7. Assuming Euodia was one of the "complainers" in the church, how do you think the examples of Timothy and Epaphroditus affected her? How do they affect you?

Answers will vary. Most often, those who put others needs before their own become role models for those who surround them.

1. Can you relate to the feelings of Euodia? On the scale below, rate how

This question may help group members realize that they are not alone in their hardships. Encourage participants to be honest and vulnerable about their answers. Use this question to spark conversation about ways to find joy in the midst of all that is going on around you.

2. Think about the lives of the following people in the Bible. How did they find and express joy when their circumstances were unpleasant?

Take time with your group to go over this list as these biblical examples will be an encouragement to them as they seek to express joy in an unpleasant time. You may encourage members of your group to write these examples down in an easily accessible place as an encouragement in future times of stress or discomfort.

3. Read Matthew 7:11. What promises are there for a child of God? How does this promise affect the bad things you are facing?

Each person in your group may have a different interpretation on this scripture depending on their personal stories. Remind group members that God is invested in every detail of their lives. He has their best interest in mind in every situation, even when they seem grim.

4. Do you have a favorite song or hymn that draws you closer to God? Write the words to the song here. Take a moment to reflect on each phrase. Now, sing it to the Lord in worship.

Answers will vary. While you may not want each group member to sing the songs or hymns that they have chosen, it may be a good idea to have each person share a lyric and why it is so meaningful to them.

5. Why do you feel God sometimes allows you to go through difficult situations? What are some lessons you learned when you were going through unpleasant experiences in the past?

This question is designed to create some deep reflection. Encourage honest conversation about unpleasant experiences people in your group have walked through and the lessons they learned from them.

6. Take a moment to read Galatians 5:22-23. How is joy a result of walking with God? How do prayer, Bible study, church attendance, and worship affect your walk with the Lord?

This passage reveals to us that joy is a fruit of the Spirit of the Lord. We are also created to be a part of the body of Christ. We are meant to fellowship with each other every day. If we stop encouraging, stop building each other up in Christ, then our hearts can grow hard.

1. Complete this sentence: My goal in life is to...

Answers for this will vary. Often, our goal and our purpose are the same thing. Encourage the members of your group to find their purpose and pursue it with all they have.

2. Think of your favorite competitive sport. How would you describe a perfect athlete in that sport? How would that athlete describe a perfect game? How does the discipline and training to become an athlete who has perfected that sport compare to the Christian life?

Again, answers for this will vary. Often, those who are the best at their particular sport train hard to be the very best that they can be. Training is often grueling and unpleasant but the athletes persevere for the sake of reaching their goals.

3. Read Philippians 3:13. In your own words, complete these sentences:

Thinking about your past, Paul said you should <u>forget it.</u>
Thinking of your future, Paul said you should <u>push forward.</u>

4. The Bible uses powerful word pictures to demonstrate the forgiveness of God. Read each of these verses and write what your Heavenly Father did with your sins when He forgave you.

Psalm 103:12 – He removed them as far as the east is from the west.
Isaiah 38:17 – He delivered our lives from the pit of destruction, casting our sins behind his back.
Micah 7:19 – He cast our sins into the depths of the sea.

5. Write a prayer of gratitude to God for forgiving your sins. Try to think of another word picture you can use to express how you feel about forgiven sins.

Depending on how well the group knows each other, consider inviting people to read their prayers aloud if they are comfortable. Pray one united prayer asking God to remind your group that no matter how bad their sins may be, they are forgiven.

6. Read Hebrews 12:1-2. The writer of Hebrews also compared the Christian life to a runner in a race. To succeed, it is important for you to put away every distraction in your life that takes your eyes off Jesus. What are some things you need to consider putting out of your life to help you grow as a believer?

While this exercise is designed as a form of self reflection, you may want to highlight the areas that members mention that overlap. Use these as a form of unity amongst the group.

7. In Hebrews 12:1-2, the writer encourages you to look at the models of godliness in your life. Who are some people that you view as mature, godly people? Why? How might you encourage them to spend more time with you and help you grow in your Christian life?

This question helps ground the discussion in practical application. If we want to grow deeper in our own faith, we must walk with and model those who are grounded deep in their faith.

8. Read Philippians 3:20-21. Paul often mentions our bodies as temporary when encouraging spiritual maturity. How do your thoughts about your human body affect your spiritual maturity? How can an obsession with your body hinder your spiritual growth?

Answers will vary. Encourage members in your group who may be farther along in age that their contributions to the body of Christ are more important in their current stage of life than ever. Their wisdom is a gift for those who are following in their footsteps.

WEEK 7 : VALUE YOUR RELATIONSHIPS

1. How have you seen or heard of ways people get offended in church? How did it affect their lives and the effectiveness of the church?

Answers will vary. The enemy knows that the church is strongest when its members are united. That is why he often attacks by trying to break relationships.

2. What are some areas where two Christians who love Christ can disagree? How can these disagreements cause friction between two people? What keeps people from agreeing to disagree on the minor things while they work together for the important things?

Again, answers will vary. Remind members in your group that even in small disagreements, the body of Christ is best when it can find common ground to stand upon.

3. Read Matthew 5:23-26. If you know someone is upset because of something you did, what are you to do? If you are upset with someone for something they did, what are you to do?

This passage is a good reminder that we should move toward forgiveness and reconciliation as quickly as possible so that we can come to our Lord with clean hearts. It is important to keep in mind that some members in your group may be walking through times of hurt that are harder to forgive than others. Be sensitive to their situation.

4. Do you know two believers who have experienced conflict? What are some ways you could help the two reconcile with each other?

Answers to this will vary.

5. Read Philippians 4:5. Paul told the Philippians to let their "reasonableness" be known to everyone. Circle the words below that describe a reasonable person?

A reasonable person is patient, kind, thoughtful, sensitive, understanding, and a good listener. It may also be a good idea to review the fruits of the Spirit when discussing what it looks like to be a reasonable person.

6. How does thanking God for the good qualities of the people in your life help you minimize areas of conflict?

Answers will vary. Often times thanking God for good qualities in people not only serves as a form of thanksgiving, but it also gives us a way for us to reflect on what makes that person such a godly person as we strive to be godly people ourselves.

1. Make a list of everything worry achieves (if you can think of one!). Now make a list of everything you witnessed prayer achieving. How does anxiety or worry take away peace? How does prayer calm our hearts?

This is a powerful exercise that will show members in your group the power of prayer and how wasteful worry is.

2. How do negative thoughts or impure thoughts affect you and your actions?

Answers will vary. Remind members of your group that impure thoughts occupy space that should be taken up by pure thoughts. One can't be pure if their thoughts are lustful. One cannot be lovely if their thoughts are rooted in gossip.

3. Paul spoke of times when he had plenty and times when he didn't. Write a brief summary of a time when you struggled financially, and write about a time when you had plenty. What did you learn from both situations?

Encourage participants to be honest and vulnerable. This question has the potential to allow members of your group to see that they are not alone in their struggles. Stories of victory that arise from this discussion will also serve as an encouragement to those in your group.

4. Make a list of the things you need to do to be a successful Christ follower. As you make your list, remember there are some things you might need that aren't tangible, such as patience. Be sure to include them.

Each participants' list will look different. Remind your group members that their list is their launch pad for being a successful Christ follower.

5. Complete this sentence:
"I believe God is calling me to _____."

This exercise will give members of your group their "next steps" toward what God is calling them to do. Encourage the members of your group to write these steps somewhere other than this book, that is accessible on a daily basis, as a reminder of their calling and what they need to do to fulfill it.

6. What are the benefits of giving? How has God blessed you, and how have you grown spiritually by giving?

Answers will vary depending on each participants spiritual walk.

7. As you conclude this study, what is an area where you feel you need to "rise up" and spiritually overcome? What have you discovered in this study that will help you do it?

Again, answers will vary. Try to encourage each member of your group share one or two things that they have learned through this study that will help them to rise up.

WOMEN OF JOY™

A calling that turned into a conference - Women of Joy has been changing the lives of women since 1993. Led by Debbie and Phil Waldrep, these weekends serve and minister to thousands of women from all over the country who gather for one purpose: Jesus.

To learn more visit **womenofjoy.org**